SMART ABOUT SPORTS

Meet the Bears

By
Mike Kennedy
with Mark Stewart

NORWOOD HOUSE PRESS

Norwood House Press, P.O. Box 316598, Chicago, Illinois 60631

For information regarding Norwood House Press,
please visit our website at: www.norwoodhousepress.com or call 866-565-2900.

Photo Credits:
Getty Images (4, 7, 8, 12, 13, 16, 20, 21), Associated Press (15, 18, 23).
Cover Photos:
   Top Left: Fleer Corp; Top Right: Doug Pensinger/Getty Images; Bottom Left: Jonathan Daniel/Getty Images;
   Bottom Right: Leaf Gum Co.
The football memorabilia photographed for this book is part of the authors' collection:
   Page 6) Dixie Cup Co., Inc., Page 10) Red Grange: The Goudey Gum Co.; Bill George: Topps, Inc.; Mike Ditka:
   Topps, Inc.; Sid Luckman: Leaf Gum Co., Page 11) Dick Butkus: Topps, Inc.; Walter Payton:
   Crane Potato Chip; Brian Urlacher: Fleer Corp.; Mike Singletary: Fleer Corp., Page 22) Red Label Records.
Special thanks to Topps, Inc.

Editor: Brian Fitzgerald
Designer: Ron Jaffe
Project Management: Black Book Partners, LLC.
Editorial Production: Jessica McCulloch

LIBRARY OF CONGRESS CATALOGING-IN-PUBLICATION DATA
   Kennedy, Mike, 1965-
   Meet the Bears / by Mike Kennedy with Mark Stewart.
        p. cm. -- (Smart about sports)
   Includes bibliographical references and index.
   Summary: "An introductory look at the Chicago Bears football team.
   Includes a brief history, facts, photos, records, glossary, and fun
   activities"--Provided by publisher.
    ISBN-13: 978-1-59953-393-3 (library edition : alk. paper)
    ISBN-10: 1-59953-393-6 (library edition : alk. paper)
   1. Chicago Bears (Football team)--Juvenile literature. I. Stewart, Mark,
   1960- II. Title.
    GV956.C5K46 2011
    796.332'640977311--dc22
                              2010005790

Manufactured in the United States of America in North Mankato, Minnesota.
156N–072010

Contents

Words in **bold type** are defined on page 24.

Victory! The Bears win a trip to the Super Bowl.

The Chicago Bears

The Chicago Bears love the cold and wind. So do their fans. The Bears play well in snow and ice. They are at their best when the weather is at its worst.

Once Upon a Time

A man named George Halas started the Bears. They were one of the first teams to join the National Football League (NFL). The Bears have always put great players on the field. Bronko Nagurski and Walter Payton were two of the best.

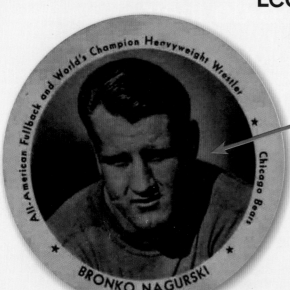

Walter Payton loved playing for the Bears.

The fans watch a game at Soldier Field.

At the Stadium

The Bears play their home
games at Soldier Field.
It is near Lake Michigan.
Sometimes, fog rolls in.
The Bears don't mind.
They are used to playing
in bad weather.

Shoe Box

The cards on these pages belong to the authors. They show some of the best Bears ever.

Red Grange

Running Back/ Defensive Back
- 1925 & 1929–1934
Red Grange was called the "Galloping Ghost." He was very fast.

Bill George

Linebacker
- 1952–1965
Bill George was the leader of the team's defense.

Sid Luckman

Quarterback
- 1939–1950
In the 1940s, Sid Luckman helped the Bears win four titles.

Mike Ditka

Tight End
- 1961–1966
Mike Ditka won one title as a player with the Bears. He won another as their coach.

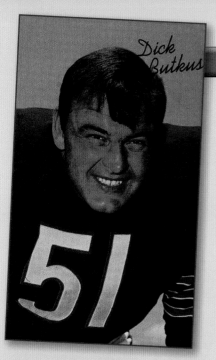

Dick Butkus

Linebacker • 1965–1973
No one tackled harder than Dick Butkus.

Walter Payton

Running Back • 1975–1987
Walter Payton was a great runner. Fans called him "Sweetness."

Mike Singletary

Linebacker • 1981–1992
Mike Singletary made sure the Bears always played their best.

Brian Urlacher

Linebacker • 2000–
Brian Urlacher was named the NFL's best defensive player in 2005.

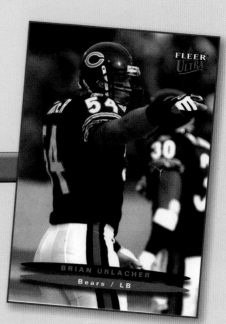

ABC's
of
Football

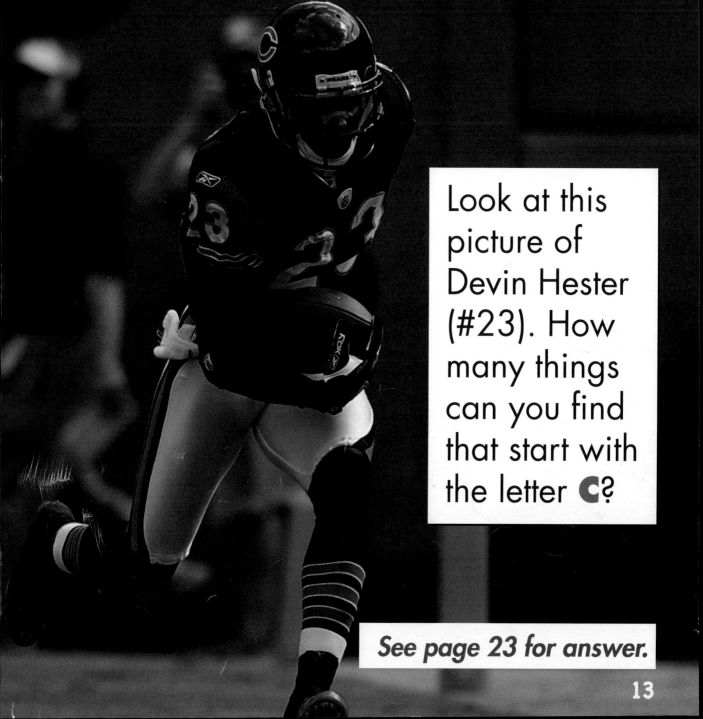

Look at this picture of Devin Hester (#23). How many things can you find that start with the letter **C**?

See page 23 for answer.

Brain Games

Here is a poem about a famous Bear:

There once was a runner named Sayers,
With talent in layers and layers.
Because of his speed,
And great moves indeed,
He outran all other players.

Guess which one of these facts is **TRUE**:

- *Gale Sayers scored six* **touchdowns** *in a game.*

- *Gale played linebacker for the Bears.*

See page 23 for answer.

14

Anything could happen when Gale Sayers had the ball.

15

Staley waves to the fans before a game.

Fun on the Field

The Bears have a mascot named Staley. He is named after the team's first owner. Staley loves to dance for the fans.

On the Map

The Bears call Chicago, Illinois home.
The players come from all over the world.
These Bears made the **All-Pro** team.
Match each with the place he was born:

1 **Bronko Nagurski** • All-Pro in 1932-1934 & 1936
Rainy River, Ontario, Canada

2 **Rick Casares** • All-Pro in 1956
Tampa, Florida

3 **Doug Atkins** • All-Pro in 1963
Humboldt, Tennessee

4 **Dan Hampton** • All-Pro in 1984
Oklahoma City, Oklahoma

5 **Richard Dent** • All-Pro in 1985
Atlanta, Georgia

United States Map

The Bears play in Chicago, Illinois.

World Map

What's in the Locker?

The team's home uniform has a dark blue jersey. It almost looks black. The Bears sometimes wear an orange jersey instead.

Lance Briggs wears the team's home uniform.

The team's road
uniform has a
white jersey.
For all games,
the team wears
a dark blue
helmet. It has an
orange letter C
on both sides.

Jay Cutler wears the
team's road uniform.

We Won!

The Bears won their first NFL title in 1921. They won their eighth in 1985. That was their best season. The Bears even made a rap song that year. It was called "The **Super Bowl** Shuffle."

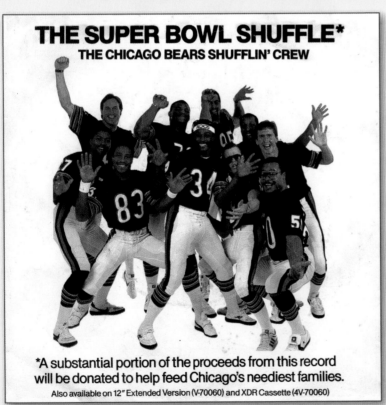

THE SUPER BOWL SHUFFLE*
THE CHICAGO BEARS SHUFFLIN' CREW

*A substantial portion of the proceeds from this record will be donated to help feed Chicago's neediest families.

Also available on 12" Extended Version (V-70060) and XDR Cassette (4V-70060)

The Bears show off their dance moves.

Record Book

These Bears stars set team records.

Running Back	Record	Year
Gale Sayers	22 total touchdowns	1965
Walter Payton	1,852 **yards**	1984

Quarterback/Receiver	Record	Year
Ken Kavanaugh	13 touchdown catches	1947
Dick Gordon	13 touchdown catches	1970
Erik Kramer	29 touchdown passes	1995
Marty Booker	100 catches	2001

Answer for ABC's of Football

Here are some words in the picture that start with **C***: Chicago Uniform, Chin Strap, Cleats. Did you find any others?*

Answer for Brain Games

The first fact is true. Gale Sayers scored six times in a 1965 game. He played running back for the Bears.

Football Words

ALL-PRO
An honor given to the best players at each position.

SUPER BOWL
The game that decides the champion of the NFL.

TOUCHDOWNS
Scoring plays worth six points.

YARDS
A yard is a distance of three feet. A football field is 100 yards from goal line to goal line.

Index

Photos are on **bold** numbered pages.

About the Bears

Learn more about the Bears at www.chicagobears.com

Learn more about football at www.profootballhof.com

24